CW00853895

The
Young
Vegetarian's
A-Z

Scholastic Children's Books,
Scholastic Publications Ltd,
7–9 Pratt Street, London NW1 0AE, UK

Scholastic Inc.,
730 Broadway, New York, NY 10003, USA

Scholastic Canada Ltd,
123 Newkirk Road, Richmond Hill,
Ontario, Canada L4C 3G5

Ashton Scholastic Pty Ltd,
PO Box 579, Gosford, New South Wales,
Australia

Ashton Scholastic Ltd,
Private Bag 1, Penrose, Auckland 6,
New Zealand

Published by Scholastic Publications Ltd, 1992

Text copyright © Debra Shipley, 1992

Illustrations copyright © Jane Campkin, 1992

ISBN 0 590 55019 5

THE Young Vegetarian's A-Z

by

Debra Shipley

Illustrated by Jane Campkin

Hippo Books
Scholastic Children's Books
London

For
Janet Selby

...lentils...

- Thank you, Helen Greathead, for making this book happen and for giving me some of your recipes when I got stuck! Any more ideas for the letter U?
- Thank you, Simon Molesworth, for giving me lots of help by eating and cooking vegetarian food.

Know-How

Veggie you

Whether you're a confirmed vegetarian, a recent convert or just thinking about it, information about vegetarian food is often either non-existent or difficult to understand.

This book aims to be different, because it tells you what you really want to know, like what to do if you're the only vegetarian in your family. It describes all the usual foods vegetarians eat and introduces some of the more unusual, explains ways of preparing and cooking food and gives plenty of tasty recipes for you to try out. Issues such as the use of pesticides and factory farming are raised and terms such as nutrition, minerals and fibre are explained. Under Questions some answers to meat-eaters' most constant queries are offered.

Hands on!

Suppose you want to know about Tofu, just look it up as you would in a dictionary:

Tofu is used quite a lot in Japanese cookery. It's made from SOYA beans . . .

Know-How

..Know how...

Words in capitals are cross-referenced elsewhere. So if you want to know about SOYA – just look it up. All main entries are given in capitals and everything is organized alphabetically, apart from the menus which come at the end of the section they are listed under.

You the cook

This book dares you to cook vegetarian meals for yourself, your friends and your family. That means experimenting with a whole variety of vegetarian foods. If you haven't tasted some of the ingredients given in this book (such as bean sprouts, carob, hummus or tahini), give them a go. If you think you don't like something (such as garlic or olives), give it a second chance – you might just love it in a vegetarian dish.

Cooking can be fun. However, sometimes things can go wrong. It happens to the greatest of chefs, so don't be put off if you make a mistake. Do be careful in the kitchen, and make sure an adult knows what you are doing.

Finally, all the recipes in the book are easy, but if you've never cooked before ask someone to help you the first few times.

Go for it!

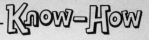

Thanks go to the organizations below, who have supplied excellent information. If you want to know more about any of them, write to them at these addresses:

- **ARK** (campaigns on environmental issues such as the greenhouse effect) 498 Harrow Road, London W9 3QA
- **Friends of the Earth** 26–28 Underwood Street, London N1 7JQ
- **The Vegetarian Society** Parkdale, Dunham Road, Altrincham, Chesire, WA14 4QG

Debra Shipley 1991

Additives are present in loads of prepared foods. When did you last see a real orange that had juice anything like the colour of orange squash? Never. That's because squash is coloured with an additive called tartrazine, which is labelled as an E number on the squash bottle. Food colourings are labelled E100–E180, so look out for them on the labels of your food and drink.

But are additives dangerous? Some people think they are, some do not. So perhaps it's best to play safe and avoid as many as you

can by eating and drinking as much additive-free food as possible. That means saying 'no' to most soft drinks and 'yes' to pure fruit juice; 'no' to many processed foods and 'yes' to fresh vegetables; 'no' to FAST FOOD and 'yes' to wholesome homemade dishes.

Agar-Agar is made from SEAWEED. It's a good substitute for gelatine if you want to make a fruit mousse or a jelly.

Agriculture, and farming in general, is geared towards increasing production. In animal farming this has led to FACTORY FARMING, and in crop farming it has led to extensive use of PESTICIDES and fertilizers. In addition, to press as much land as possible into use for farming, part of the countryside has been damaged. For example, hedges have been destroyed and soil has been eroded. Many countries in Europe have what is known as a 'food mountain'. This is the term given to the huge amount of food which is stored in enormous warehouses because it is not needed to feed the people of the country in which it is produced. Some groups of people, such as Friends of the Earth (see p. 7), believe that such over-production of crops should be discouraged and that ORGANIC FARMING would help the situation.

Alfalfa is a green SALAD vegetable which tastes a bit like cress. Try tossing it in VINAIGRETTE.

...alfalfa...

A

Animals are not eaten by vegetarians. Sounds obvious, doesn't it? OK, you'd know a pork chop for what it is – a lump of pig – but what about a raspberry jelly? Many brands of fruit jelly contain a bit of animal in the form of gelatine, which is made from animal bones. So, if you want to avoid eating animals in any form, start to read product labels carefully.

..recipe...

Apple Snow (for 4)
450g (1lb) cooking apples
1 tablespoon clear HONEY
2 free-range EGG whites*
1 dessertspoon chopped NUTS

1) Wash, peel and core the apples then cut them into roughly 2cm chunks.
2) Put the chopped apple and the honey into a saucepan with a little water (just enough to cover the bottom of the pan). Cover the pan with a lid, then cook until the apples are soft and pulpy.
3) Leave the cooked apples until they are completely cold (this takes about 2 hours).
4) Whisk the egg whites until they make stiff peaks.
5) Add the egg whites gently to the apple mixture. It's important not to stir the mixture too much or the 'snow' will 'melt'.
6) To serve, tip the apple snow into a glass dish and sprinkle with the chopped nuts.

* To separate the white of an egg from the yolk, crack the egg and break it gently, so that the yolk stays in the shell. Pour the white into one bowl and the yolk into another.

Aubergine is also known as egg plant, though this vegetable has nothing to do with eggs! Dark purple and glossy, aubergines are used in a lot of Mediterranean dishes. Try frying thin slices in olive OIL. They soak up a lot of oil, so when they're cooked (soft and brown), drain them on kitchen paper. Serve with a blob of Greek YOGHURT.

...eggplant...

Avocado is a green (sometimes blotchy green and brown) pear-shaped fruit with a large stone. It comes from America and the West Indies, but is now grown in large quantities in Israel too. Its outer skin is tough and can't be eaten, but the flesh inside, which is soft when ripe and pale green, is delicious. (See PASTA.)

Bacon (See QUESTIONS, TOFU.)

Barley (also sometimes called pot barley) is a GRAIN. In its unprocessed form it's very tough and you usually have to soak it overnight before cooking. Barley used to be popular for bulking out stews, particularly during the Second World War when food was scarce. Today it's thought a bit old fashioned, but some vegetarian restaurants are beginning to use it again by making, for instance, their own barley BREAD.

Beans mean a lot more than beans on toast. Beans are PULSES and there are lots of different kinds. Look out for:
- butter beans (which are kidney-shaped and have nothing to do with butter!)
- mung beans (from which BEAN SPROUTS are usually grown)
- red kidney beans (yes, they're red and kidney-shaped)
- haricot beans (small, oval shaped and white – they're best known as baked beans)

Beans are particularly important to vegetarians because they are a good source of PROTEIN.

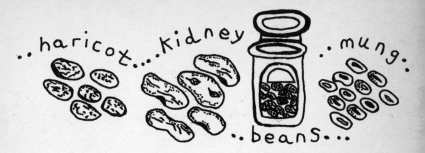

Bean sprouts have been made popular by Chinese cooking. Have you ever tried a crispy pancake roll stuffed with bean sprouts? Bean sprouts (along with sprouted GRAINS and LENTILS) are really good for you because they contain plenty of VITAMINS, MINERALS and PROTEIN. If you've never seen bean sprouts on sale in the shops near you then start your own sprouting enterprise – it's dead easy.

You need:
1 large jar
1 piece of muslin (big enough to stretch over the jar)
1 elastic band
25g (1 oz) mung beans (experiment later with other BEANS and SEEDS)
Action:
1) Put the beans into the jar.
2) Cover the beans with cold water.
3) Stretch the muslin cloth over the jar and secure with the elastic band. Leave for 12 hours.
4) Drain off the water (through the cloth).
5) Refill (again through the cloth) with clean water and shake gently. Pour out the water. Leave for 12 hours.

...beansprouts...

6) Repeat the last step twice a day until the beans sprout. This takes from two to four days. (If you forget to clean them regularly, the beans will rot. So why don't you decide to wash your beans at a particular time, such as when you clean your teeth?)

To eat:

Add your home-produced bean sprouts to a SALAD, or fry them in a little OIL and then toss them in soy sauce.

Berries are fruits which do not have a stone. The best known berries are gooseberries, raspberries, blackberries and strawberries. Ripe berries taste great on their own, but for a feast mash your favourite berries with cream and stir in broken macaroons. (If using gooseberries, stew, cool and sweeten first.) Eat while the macaroons are still crunchy.

Biscuits often contain animal fats, so check the label carefully before you buy any.

Blenders are used in cooking to liquidize food or chop it up. They're electrical gadgets so your home may not have one. A blender is definitely worth having if you're a veggie cook, as it takes so much of the effort out of food preparation. But you can use other methods, such as grating (for breadcrumbs), sieving (for soups), hand whisking (for milkshakes), or chopping the ingredients finely (for GAZPACHO). Blenders are fairly cheap so you might ask for one for a birthday present or save up and treat yourself.

Note: A blender, like all other electrical equipment, can be dangerous, so get someone to show you how to use it and **never** put your fingers into the goblet when it's plugged in, or leave it where a small child could get hold of it.

..blender.

Bran is the outside layer of the grain of wheat and is rich in fibre.

Bread comes in many different shapes, sizes and flavours. Different countries have their own favourite types of bread. Here are some of the most easily available ones to try out:

- black bread (German)
- RYE bread (German)
- baguette (French)
- pitta bread (Greek)
- nan bread (Indian)

15

...bread....

...baguette..

...nan..

...pitta...

Bread is also a useful cooking ingredient:

- as crumbs (made by putting slices of bread into a food processor or BLENDER for a few seconds) which can be used to make savoury stuffing (see XMAS);
- as a soup thickener – just add a slice to any soup which is being blended and it will be instantly thicker;
- as a croûton (a savoury 'biscuit' to float on soup) – just cut the bread into 2cm cubes and fry in OIL with some crushed GARLIC until golden brown.

Buckwheat is often classified as a GRAIN but it is, in fact, a SEED. It can be bought in either natural or toasted form and can be substituted for RICE in dishes such as VEGETABLE CURRY.

Bulgur is sometimes known as 'cracked wheat', because that's exactly what it is – wheat which has been cracked open and steamed. It's eaten a lot in Middle Eastern countries.

...menu...

Bean Bolognese (for 2)
This is a quick tomato-flavoured sauce which you can serve on top of any kind of PASTA.

a little cooking OIL
1 onion, chopped
1 clove of GARLIC, crushed
2 large carrots, washed and grated
1 dessertspoon tomato purée
1 small tin chopped tomatoes
1 small tin butter BEANS, drained and washed
grated CHEESE or chopped HERBS to decorate

1) Heat the oil in a medium pan.
2) Add the onion and cook gently for about five minutes.
3) Add the garlic and carrot, and stir well to coat with the oil.
4) Put a lid on the pan and cook very gently for 5 minutes.
5) Stir in the tomato purée and chopped tomatoes (add a little water if the sauce seems too dry).
6) Cover with lid and cook for 15 minutes.
7) Add butter beans and cook, without lid, for 5 minutes.
8) Add salt and pepper if you want to.
9) Serve on pasta and sprinkle with grated cheese or chopped herbs.

Banana Hissle (for 2)

This pudding gets its name from the sound that the bananas make while they're cooking!

2 bananas
25g (1 oz) margarine
2 dessertspoons golden syrup

1) Slice the bananas lengthways.
2) Heat the margarine gently in a small frying pan until it begins to make a 'hissle' sound.
3) Add the sliced banana and cook (keeping the pan 'hissling') for 2–3 minutes.
4) Stir in the golden syrup and heat through.
5) Serve immediately!

Carob powder is made from the crushed seeds of the carob pod and is used as a substitute for chocolate. It doesn't taste too much like the real thing, but try it and see – you may like it. It contains VITAMINS A, B and D as well as the MINERALS calcium and phosphorus.

Cereal (See GRAIN.)

Cheese is a milk product usually made with animal RENNET, but a vegetarian version is now widely available, so check labels before buying.

···cheese···

...recipe...

Cheese Soufflé (for 4)

Soufflés have a bad reputation – everyone seems to think they're hard to make. Well, they're easy if you know how. The real tricks of the trade are a hot oven and hungry people ready and waiting at the table *before* you remove the soufflé from the oven, so that they can see it in all its puffed-up glory before it starts to subside!*

25 g (1 oz) butter
25 g (1 oz) flour
250 ml (½ pint) MILK
50 g (2 oz) CHEESE, finely grated
1 teaspoon MUSTARD powder, mixed to a paste with a little MILK
4 free-range EGGS separated (SEE APPLE SNOW)

1) Set the oven to 190°C/375°F/Gas Mark 5 (it needs to be hot when you put the soufflé in), and grease a soufflé dish.
2) Melt the butter in a large saucepan.
3) Remove pan from heat and stir in the flour.
4) Return pan to heat and cook gently for 30 seconds.
5) Remove pan from heat and add a little milk. Stir well until there are no lumps.
6) Add a little more milk and stir well.
7) Repeat the process until all the milk has been stirred in. Don't be tempted to add the milk quickly or it will become lumpy.

8) Add the mustard paste.

9) Return pan to heat and keep stirring until the milk thickens into a smooth sauce.

10) Remove from the heat and leave to cool for 5 minutes.

11) Add the cheese and egg yolks.

12) Whisk the egg whites (in a very clean bowl) until they're stiff. Some people test for stiffness by turning the bowl upside down. If the whites are stiff enough they stay in the bowl, if not . . . well, you can guess what happens. A safer test is to see if the whites make soft peaks.

13) Stir a large spoonful of whisked egg white into the cheese sauce.

14) Add the rest of the egg white and gently fold in. You do this by making a circular movement through the sauce with a metal spoon, then folding the sauce over the egg white with a sort of slicing motion. It's easier than it sounds. Anyway, the main points are: (a) to stir as little as you can, (b) to trap the maximum amount of air.

15) Pour the soufflé mixture into the greased dish.

16) Bake in the hot oven for 25–30 minutes, until the soufflé has risen and has a firm golden-brown crust.

Serve with a green SALAD or green vegetables such as broccoli.

* The inside of the soufflé is sometimes quite runny. Don't worry – it still tastes good.

Chicory is a pale green, almost white, vegetable with tightly packed leaves. It can be cooked or used as a SALAD ingredient.

Chilli peppers are used to add a fiery flavour to dishes. The well-known dish Chilli con Carne (chilli with meat) comes from Mexico, but you can make an even better vegetarian version – Chilli sin Carne (chilli without meat!)

...recipe...

Chilli sin Carne (for 4)

1 small red PEPPER, chopped and de-seeded
1 small green pepper, chopped and de-seeded
1 medium onion, chopped
1 clove GARLIC, crushed
¼ teaspoon chilli powder*
400 g (15 oz) tin tomatoes
400 g (15 oz) tin red kidney BEANS
1 tablespoon vegetable or olive OIL

1) Fry the onions, garlic and peppers for a few minutes in the oil until soft.
2) Add chilli powder.
3) Drain the beans and add to the pan with tomatoes.
4) Gently mix the ingredients, roughly chopping the tomatoes.
5) Bring to the boil and simmer gently for 30 minutes, stirring from time to time.
6) Add salt and pepper if you want.
7) Serve with brown RICE and a blob of natural yoghurt.

* Be careful when you use chilli peppers or powder. It can be very hot! Make sure you wash your hands as soon as you have used it, and do not touch your face or eyes. If you should get some in your eye, wash it quickly in cold water and, if it is still painful, consult a doctor.

Christmas (See XMAS.)

Chutney (See RELISH.)

Coleslaw is a salad made from sliced raw white cabbage mixed with mayonnaise. Make your own by slicing 50 g (2 oz) white cabbage very finely. Add a dollop of mayonnaise and stir well. That's all there is to it! Now experiment a bit by adding sultanas, chopped apple, chopped NUTS or grated carrots.

Corn is the term often given to crops of GRAIN. It's also the American word for SWEETCORN. The hard variety of corn can be cooked in OIL, when it explodes it forms popcorn!

Courgette (See ZUCCHINI.)

Couscous is made from crushed wheat. It's used mainly in North Africa, where it's steamed over a pot of vegetable stew.

Crudités is a fancy name for a selection of raw vegetables which are served with dips such as HUMMUS. Carrots, celery, peppers, mushrooms, radishes, spring onions, cucumber, ZUCCHINI, CHICORY leaves and cauliflower are all good for dunking.

Dal is a LENTIL dish which comes from India. (See INDIAN VEGETAR-IAN FOOD.)

Dandelion leaves can be eaten as a salad – honestly! Pick young shoots as the leaves get tougher as they grow bigger. But choose your plants carefully (make sure that there haven't been any dogs or cats around) and wash them well. Watch out if you've been raiding the hedgerows, they might have been sprayed with PESTICIDES.

Diet does not, in this book, ever mean slimming. If you seriously think you have a weight problem, see your doctor. She/he is the person qualified to advise you. Diet, in this book, refers to a balanced and healthy eating pattern, which means reasonable amounts of a wide variety of foods: plenty of fresh vegetables and fruits along with EGGS, NUTS, PULSES and CHEESE. If in doubt, ask an expert (your doctor) and don't get conned by food fads in magazines.

Dried fruits are often much sweeter than fresh, because the fruit is left longer on the tree to ripen. They're a good source of

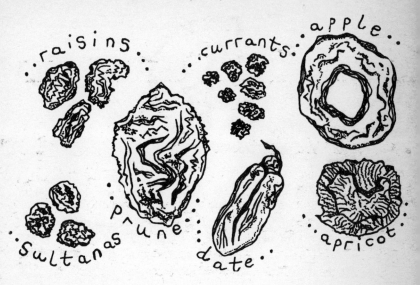

·· dried fruit ···

raisins · · · currants · · · apple ··

·· sultanas · · prune · · date ·· · apricot

MINERALS and VITAMINS. Useful in cooking, they can also be eaten as a snack instead of, say, crisps. Here are some of the best known dried fruits:

- apples – grown in Britain;
- apricots – originally from Asia, but now grown in large quantities in South Africa and Australia;
- currants – grown as tiny purple grapes, mainly in Greece;
- dates – from North Africa;
- prunes – grown as plums in America;
- raisins – grown as grapes in Spain, Australia, South Africa and America;
- sultanas – grown as white grapes in Turkey, Australia and South Africa.

Dried Fruit — Date Discoveries

If you're invited to a party, and worried about some of the food you'll have to eat, you could volunteer to bring your own. Even non-veggie friends will love these tasty mouthfuls.

12 large dates
3 tablespoons cream cheese
2 teaspoons chopped chives
¼ teaspoon curry powder

1) Cut the dates in half lengthways. Remove the stones.
2) Mix together the cheese, chives and curry powder.
3) Place a teaspoon-sized blob of cheese mixture between the two date halves, making a sort of sandwich.
4) Serve the Date Discoveries on a plate and let people help themselves.

Egg plant (See AUBERGINE.)

Eggs form an important part of a vegetarian's diet (unless you're a VEGAN). But it's important to eat only eggs which are labelled 'free-range'. Eggs are also labelled 'farm eggs', 'fresh eggs', and 'farm fresh eggs', but these all refer to eggs which have been produced in battery or FACTORY FARMS. Free-range is a term given to eggs produced by hens which have not been confined in cruel battery conditions.

...recipe...

Eggs and Cheese Sauce (for 4)

4 free-range eggs

25 g (1 oz) margarine

25 g (1 oz) flour

½ teaspoon English mustard powder, mixed to a paste with a little WATER

250 ml (½ pint) MILK

100 g (4 oz) CHEESE, grated

1) Hardboil the eggs in water for 10 minutes.

2) Carefully take the eggs out of the boiling water and put them into a bowl of cold water for about 10 minutes (this stops a black ring forming around the yolk and makes them easier to shell).

3) Shell the eggs, slice them in half lengthways, and put them on a greased oven-proof dish.

4) To make the sauce, gently melt the margarine in a saucepan.

5) Turn off the heat and then add the flour and mustard. Stir well with a wooden spoon.

6) Add the milk a little at a time (don't be tempted to hurry or you'll end up with a lumpy sauce).

7) When all the milk has been carefully blended into the flour turn on the heat again and keep stirring until the sauce thickens.
8) Add ¾ of the cheese and stir until it melts into the sauce.
9) Pour the cheese sauce over the eggs and scatter the rest of the cheese over the top.
10) Put the dish under a hot grill until the cheese bubbles and turns golden brown.
11) Serve with a green SALAD.

Enchilada is a stuffed TORTILLA served with a CHILLI sauce. It's traditionally stuffed with meat, but fashionable restaurants sometimes offer vegetarian versions.

Endive is a frilly-leaved vegetable used in SALADS, particularly in France where it's very popular. It has a strong flavour, but give it a go – it's interesting.

Factory farming means money. Packing animals into limited space, making it impossible for them to move much, controlling the amount of light and food they are given, all make for more profit. The sad thing is that, as this book shows, there is no need whatsoever for humans to eat animals. Once packaged and on supermarket shelves, pigs, chickens, calves and lambs don't look like animals at all, they're just lumps of MEAT to be eaten by people who can't (or don't want to) make the link between a living creature and what's on their plate. Here are a few rather disturbing facts which farmers and supermarkets don't tell customers:

- VEAL calves are kept in darkness to make their flesh white – the whiter it is, the more it's worth.
- Pigs are very intelligent, yet they're tied so that they can hardly move. Many go mad.
- Battery chickens have their beaks removed so that they can't peck themselves and each other to pieces in their tiny cramped cages.
- ANIMALS sent to slaughter houses are meant, by law, to be stunned for seven seconds before they are killed. It is known that this doesn't always happen. The RSPCA reported that 6.6

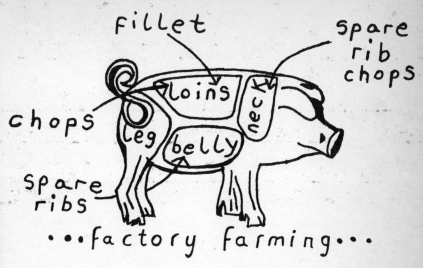

fillet

spare rib chops

loins

neck

chops

leg

belly

spare ribs

•••factory farming•••

per cent of all animals, and a huge 53 per cent of young bulls, are not properly stunned. This means that thousands of animals are suffering.

- Cows develop such a strong bond with their calves that they will push their way through barbed wire to be with them. For this reason, calves are often taken from their mothers just one day after birth.

Fast food is boring. It's expensive. It's overpackaged, which is bad for the environment and it's rarely vegetarian. OK, you can have a veggie pizza, but is the CHEESE used for the topping made with vegetarian RENNET? Probably not. You can have a Chinese take-away, but what are the chances of vegetarian STOCK being used for that thick gravy? You can, of course, have chips without fish, but they are fried in the same OIL (usually from beef). Burgers are obviously out (see MEAT). So, fast food isn't fun.

Felafel are small chick-pea fritters which are sold from street stalls in Israel, where they're considered FAST FOOD. However, unlike most take-aways, felafel are both vegetarian and NUTRITIOUS. They're served stuffed into pitta BREAD with shredded lettuce and a dollop of YOGHURT. As felafel tend to be wrapped in only the minimum of paper, they don't present too much of a threat to the environment either.

You can buy felafel in some supermarkets, but they're not nearly as good as the real street food.

Fennel has two parts – leaf and bulb – which are eaten in different ways. Fennel leaf is a HERB which has a light aniseed flavour. Fennel bulb also has an aniseed taste. It looks a bit like a misshapen onion and is eaten as a vegetable. It can be cooked or eaten raw (it gives an interesting flavour to SALADS).

Fibre, which forms the cell walls of all plants such as NUTS, GRAINS, vegetables, fruits, PULSES and BERRIES, is thought to be an important part of a well-balanced DIET.

Fish (See QUESTIONS, p. 77).

..recipe...

Fruit Salad (for 2)
This is a no-cook pudding. Anyone can make it.

1 banana, peeled and cut into thinnish slices
1 apple, washed, cored and cut into chunks
16 cherries, washed and stones removed
1 orange, peeled and cut into chunks
125 ml (¼ pint) pineapple JUICE

1) Mix all the prepared fruit together.
2) Add the fruit juice.
3) Serve with cream or natural YOGHURT.

33

Gardening isn't just for oldies – it's for you too. If you have a window-ledge you can grow your own fresh HERBS, and if you have a balcony you can grow your own strawberries, tomatoes and runner beans. However, if you have access to a plot of land why not cultivate a small kitchen garden? It's a lot more fun than you might think, and you can be sure that your vegetables have been grown a vegetarian's way – a way that doesn't use fertilizers made from dried animal blood, fish and bone meal or manure from FACTORY FARMS. On the subject of fertilizers, if you do start a garden, avoid using peat in it. Peat bogs might look like nothing much, but they have a unique ecology and are home to many rare plants and ANIMALS.

Once you get into gardening you'll be able to create fertilizer from your own compost heap. In the meantime, you could use manure from a stables. If you want to know more make for your local garden centre, or the gardening section of your local library.

Garlic is a plant which is used in cooking because it has a strong flavour. It also has a strong smell and some people have a 'thing' about eating it because they're afraid of having smelly breath! If you're one of them, try chewing some fresh parsley after eating it and do persevere – garlic is extremely good for you!

It's easy to grow, too – break a garlic bulb into individual cloves and plant them. Each will produce an interesting flower and a complete new bulb!

Garlic bread is simple to make. Cut a French stick into 2 cm pieces. Butter each piece on both sides, but keep them in the right order. Next, chop up four or five cloves of garlic. Put a bit of chopped garlic onto each slice of bread and reassemble the loaf. Wrap it tightly in foil and put it into a hot oven for about 20 minutes. It smells and tastes wonderful!

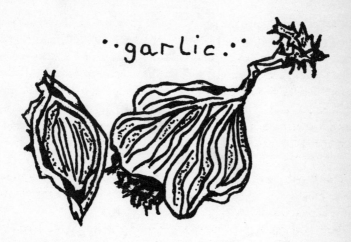

··garlic.··

Grain is a collective term given to the fruit or SEED of a cereal such as RICE, BARLEY, CORN, MILLET, OAT, RYE and wheat. In many non-western countries grain forms what is known as the 'staple' diet, which means that it forms a large part of the nation's daily food intake. Grain combined with PULSES provides a very good source of vegetarian protein.

Green Salad (for 4)

This is the most useful and the easiest dish to make.

4 lettuce leaves, washed
8 sprigs of watercress, washed
4 SPINACH leaves, washed

Make sure you shake as much WATER off the leaves as you can. Then just pile the leaves on top of each other in a bowl and mix them together. Add a VINAIGRETTE.

This is a really international menu, for four people, with dishes from three different countries!

Gazpacho

Gazpacho is a Spanish soup which is served very cold. It's made from ingredients which are typical of Mediterranean cooking – tomatoes, olive OIL, PEPPERS and cucumber – and it's simple to make.

½ slice wholemeal BREAD
½ cucumber, finely chopped
1 green pepper, finely chopped
1 small clove GARLIC, finely chopped
pinch of CHILLI powder (see * p. 22)

400 g (15 oz) tin tomatoes
1 dessertspoon wine vinegar
1 dessertspoon vegetable or olive oil

1) Put all the ingredients into a BLENDER
2) Blend until the mixture turns smooth and pink.
3) Leave in the fridge for 1–2 hours, or add ice cubes if you want to eat it quickly.
4) Serve with croûtons (see BREAD, pp. 15–16), chopped cucumber, onion or green pepper.

Goulash

Goulash is a Hungarian dish which is traditionally made with beef. This vegetarian version is loads better!

OIL for frying
2 onions, chopped
1 tablespoon paprika
1 dessertspoon flour
400 g (15 oz) tin chopped tomatoes
125 ml (¼ pint) vegetable STOCK
1 dessertspoon tomato purée
4 large carrots, scraped and cut into 1 cm chunks
4 medium ZUCCHINI, washed and cut into 1 cm chunks
2 large potatoes, peeled and cut into 1 cm chunks
1 red PEPPER, washed and cut into 1 cm chunks
8 button MUSHROOMS, washed and cut in half
125 ml (¼ pint) soured cream

1) Heat a little oil and fry the onion until soft.
2) Add the paprika and flour, then stir well.
3) Add the tomatoes and stir well.
4) Add vegetable stock and purée and stir well.
5) Add all the vegetables and bring to the boil.

6) Put a lid on the pan and reduce the heat so that the sauce simmers.
7) Cook for 25 minutes.
8) Remove from the heat and cool for 2 minutes, then stir in the soured cream.
9) Add salt and pepper if you want to.
10) Decorate with a little paprika and serve with RICE.

Gooseberry Fool

A traditional English summertime pudding. If you're feeding friends you can make this dish the day before, then you'll only have to worry about getting the goulash and the gazpacho right.

450 g (1 lb) ripe gooseberries
3 tablespoons sugar
6 tablespoons YOGHURT or double cream

1) Wash the gooseberries and pinch off the hard ends.
2) Put the gooseberries and sugar into a saucepan and just cover with water.
3) Heat until the water boils then simmer gently until the gooseberries begin to break up (about 15 minutes).
4) Break up the gooseberries, using a wooden spoon to crush them against the side of the pan.
5) Tip the squashed gooseberries into a dish and leave them to go cold.
6) Add the yoghurt or cream and beat well until you have a pale green cream.
7) Serve with extra cream or yoghurt, and with almond BISCUITS if you like them.

Halva is a sweet popular in Turkey and many Arab countries. Basic halva is made from sesame flour (see SEEDS) and HONEY, but almonds and pistachio NUTS are often added.

Health (See NUTRITION and DIET.)

Herbs have been used in cookery for centuries. For the twentieth-century vegetarian they're a great way to add extra flavour to food. You can use either fresh or dried herbs, but fresh tend to taste best so, why not grow some in pots on your bedroom window-ledge? Chives, parsley and mint are all fairly easy to grow (see GARDENING). Here are a few ways of eating some herbs:

- chopped chives (which have a slightly oniony flavour) can be scattered over thinly sliced cucumber and tomato for a colourful summer salad;
- mint leaves are good with hot new potatoes;
- chopped parsley tastes good mixed with hot buttered PASTA bows and grated CHEESE;
- bay leaves are good for flavouring soups and stews;
- rosemary is nice with KEBABS;
- tarragon tastes good in sauces;

- dill adds flavour to salads;
- basil tastes great fresh in a tomato salad, or dried in stews or sauces.

mint · parsley · herbs · bay · rosemary · basil · tarragon · dill · chives

Honey has had a good reputation for centuries as a health-giving food. It's even thought dead bodies were once preserved in it!

Honey is made by bees. They collect nectar from flowers and process it into honey in their stomachs! The flavour of the honey depends on which flowers the bees have visited.

Most honey sold in supermarkets is a blend of different types. It's more expensive to buy single-flower honeys, but well worth it as a taste experience!

...recipe...

Honey Milkshake (for 1)
175 ml (⅓ pint) MILK
1–2 teaspoons clear HONEY
a little grated chocolate

1) Put the honey and milk into a BLENDER. Blend for 30 seconds.
2) Pour the milk into a long glass and sprinkle with grated chocolate.

Hummus is a dip which comes from Greece. Made from chick peas, GARLIC, lemon juice, TAHINI and olive OIL. It's good served with pitta BREAD or CRUDITÉS. It's a bit of a fiddle to prepare, but can be bought ready made.

Ice cream is usually made with vegetable fat rather than cream, which is OK if you're a VEGAN. However, if you like the luxurious taste of the 'real thing', try making your own. It will cost a lot less than the shop variety.

Ice cream

2 free-range EGGS
75 g (3 oz) sugar
250 ml (½ pint) MILK
250 ml (½ pint) whipping cream

1) Whisk the eggs in a bowl.
2) Heat the sugar and milk until boiling point, stirring.
3) Slowly add the liquid to the eggs, stirring.
4) Tip everything back into the pan and put back on the heat, stirring until the mixture thickens (a couple of minutes).
5) Leave to cool.
6) Whip the cream until it is stiff and fold it into the mixture.
7) Pour into a shallow container and put in the freezer or the freezing compartment of your fridge until just beginning to crystallize (a couple of hours).
8) Scrape the ice cream into a bowl and beat till smooth, then put it back into the container and return it to the freezer.
9) Repeat the last step when the ice cream begins to crystallize again.
10) About an hour before you want to eat it, move the ice cream from the freezer into the main part of the fridge, so that it won't be rock solid!

You can adapt this basic recipe to make flavoured ice creams by adding one of the following between stages 4 and 5:

- a couple of drops of vanilla essence
- 2 tablespoons of ground coffee beans or instant coffee powder
- 2 tablespoons of cocoa powder

or by adding 250 g (8 oz) of cleaned, mashed BERRIES between stages 5 and 6.

···Indian food···

Indian vegetarian food. Becoming vegetarian means being adventurous about what you eat. Trying out foods from different countries is a great way of finding out about new foods you may not have considered eating before.

In many parts of India, a vegetarian DIET has been an important part of the culture for thousands of years. In Hindu families, some animals, such as the cow, are considered sacred, whilst others, such as the pig, are considered unclean. With the heat of the climate too, meat can rapidly go off, becoming dangerous to eat.

The basic diet consists of RICE, PULSES (usually called dal) and dairy produce, such as YOGHURT. It is extremely rich in PROTEIN.

Indian vegetarian restaurants are on the increase in the West. Many large towns and cities now have what are known as 'Bhel Poori Houses', serving a wide variety of vegetarian dishes. The meals are cheap and delicious, so do try one if you get the chance.

On the other hand, you could have a go at these basic recipes yourself at home. (See also KEDGEREE.)

Indian Dal (serves 3–4)
250 g (8 oz) split red LENTILS, washed and soaked in WATER for 1 hour
25 g (1 oz) butter
1 onion, finely chopped
1 dessertspoon mild Madras curry powder

1) Boil the lentils in the water for about 30 minutes, until they can be mashed into a paste.
2) Melt the butter and gently fry the onion until soft.
3) Stir in the curry powder and fry for one or two minutes.
4) Add the onions to the dal and mix well together.
5) Serve with Basmati RICE and coconut chutney (or cucumber raita if you prefer – see p. 97).

I

To add flavour to the rice, try adding a tablespoon each of sultanas, chopped onion and chopped cashew NUTS. Fry them together in OIL until the onion is soft, then mix in with 250 g (8 oz) cooked RICE.

To make a coconut chutney you will need:
50 g (2 oz) dessicated coconut
1 cup hot water
juice of 1 LEMON (or 2 tablespoons of lemon juice from a bottle)
½ small onion, chopped
a good pinch of CHILLI powder (see *p. 22)
a good pinch of ground ginger

1) Mix the coconut so that it soaks up the water to make a creamy paste.
2) Add the lemon juice, onion, chilli and ginger.
3) Put all the ingredients into a BLENDER and blend into a paste.

Information about vegetarianism and related matters can be obtained from the organizations listed on p. 7.

Jacket Potatoes

If you want to cook for more people, just multiply the ingredients.

1 huge potato, well scrubbed

1) Set the oven at very hot.*
2) Prick the potato all over with a fork.
3) Put it in the oven and cook for about an hour. (Test to see if it's ready by sticking a fork into it – it should be very soft inside and crisp outside).
4) When cooked, cut the potato in half and add your favourite topping. Here are some good ones:
- grated CHEESE
- YOGHURT
- mayonnaise
- HUMMUS

* If you have a microwave you can cook a potato in about 4 minutes – but oven-cooked jacket potatoes taste far better.

Juice makes a great drink. Many fruits and vegetables can be squeezed or 'juiced'. Experiment and see which you like, but don't overdo it – it's possible to drink too much! If you have a juicer you can try carrots, apples, tomatoes, strawberries or blackberries.

A BLENDER can be used to make juice-based drinks. Experiment and see what you can create. Here are a few ideas to start you off:

- YOGHURT and raspberries
- yoghurt and strawberries
- MILK and strawberries, topped with ICE CREAM
- yoghurt, milk and blackberries
- yoghurt and kiwi fruit (peeled)
- LEMON, orange and WATER
- nectarine and yoghurt

Julep is an old-fashioned name given to a sweet drink something like a modern-day squash.

Junket is a pudding made with MILK curds. Unfortunately, it's often thickened with RENNET.

Junk foods such as burgers, TV dinners and canned drinks, are a no, no, NO!

- *no* because they're usually NUTRITIONALLY ill balanced (often packed choc-a-block with sugar, fat and salt but low in VITAMINS and PROTEIN);
- *no* because they create huge amounts of waste. Just think of all those containers – cardboard cartons for fries, paper cups for shakes, wrapper and plastic box for the burger, plastic straws and cutlery – for a meal which takes just a few minutes to eat;
- *no* because the FAST FOOD industry uses large amounts of meat. If you're a vegetarian you would, of course, avoid the obvious hamburgers and beefburgers, but as fast foods tend not to have a contents label you have no quick way of discovering what your fries were fried in, or what went into the doughnut dough;
- *no* because they contribute to the destruction of the rainforests of the Amazon. Large areas of precious rainforests are being destroyed to create huge cattle ranches. It's thought that as much as 9 sq metres of rainforest are cut down to produce a single burger. Why are rainforests so important? There are many, many, reasons. Here are a few:
1) forest clearance is often done by burning. Burning releases carbon dioxide which is one of the main causes of the greenhouse effect;
2) trees soak up carbon dioxide, so we need them to combat the greenhouse effect;
3) burning the forests is thought to alter rainfall patterns, which in turn help create conditions of drought and flood;
4) trees protect the soil and without them the earth dries out;
5) rainforests contain millions of plants, animals and insects, some of which can only be found in rainforests;

6) many rainforest plants can be used in medicine, and it's likely that there are many more whose uses have yet to be discovered;

7) animals are endangered and the destruction of the rainforest is losing the world one species a day;

8) the native people of the rainforests are being driven out as big business moves in;

9) rainforests are incredibly beautiful.

··· junk food ····

Kale is a type of cabbage. It is dark green with crinkly leaves and you can use it in cooking like any other cabbage.

Kebab is, traditionally, small lumps of MEAT threaded onto a skewer and then grilled or cooked over hot coals. You can make vegetable kebabs by skewering cherry tomatoes, button MUSH-ROOMS, tiny onions and pieces of red PEPPER. Brush them with olive OIL before cooking. If you're barbecuing kebabs then throw a few sprigs of fresh rosemary on to the charcoal to make a wonderful smell of HERBS.

...recipe...

Kedgeree (for 4)

Kedgeree is a dish which originated in India but became very popular during the nineteenth century in Europe as a breakfast dish for well-off families. In the European dish the ingredients include fish, but the original Indian recipe was vegetarian. Here's a vegetarian version which you can eat at breakfast, lunch or supper.

50 g (2 oz) butter
1 large onion, chopped
225 g (8 oz) white long grain RICE
500 ml (1 pint) WATER
170 g (6 oz) strong CHEESE grated
1 small pot of Greek YOGHURT
4 tablespoons fresh parsley, chopped
3 free-range EGGS, boiled for 8 minutes, put into cold water for 10 minutes, then shelled and roughly chopped

1) Melt the butter in a large saucepan.
2) Add the onion and cook gently until soft.
3) Add the rice and water and bring to the boil.

4) Put a lid on the pan, turn the heat down and simmer for 30–40 minutes until the water has been absorbed and the rice is cooked.
5) Remove from the heat and stir in the cheese until it melts.
6) Add the yoghurt and stir well until the whole mixture is very creamy.
7) Add the parsley and stir well.
8) Add the eggs and stir gently.
9) Serve with a SALAD of sliced tomatoes.

Leather (See questions, p. 78).

...recipe...

Leek and Potato Soup (for 6)
1 tablespoon OIL
1 large onion, chopped
4 large potatoes, peeled and chopped into 2 cm chunks

450 g (1 lb) leeks, washed thoroughly and chopped into 2 cm chunks
750 ml (1½ pints) STOCK
125 ml (¼ pint) MILK

1) Heat the oil in a large saucepan.
2) Add the onion and fry gently until pale brown.
3) Add the potatoes, leeks and stock, then bring to the boil.
4) Put a lid on the pan and turn the heat down. Simmer for 20–25 minutes until the potatoes are cooked.
5) Remove the pan from the heat and tip the soup into a BLENDER.
6) Blend until creamy. Return to the saucepan and add the milk.
7) Taste the soup and add salt and pepper if you think it needs more flavour (add a little at a time and keep testing until it tastes good).
8) Heat the soup gently but don't let it boil.
9) Serve with crusty French BREAD.

Lemons are very useful in vegetarian cooking. The JUICE and the ZEST can be added to both sweet and savoury foods. Try adding a little JUICE to soup or sprinkle it on to pancakes. Mix WATER, lemon juice and HONEY together for a quick lemon drink. Use lemon juice instead of VINEGAR in a VINAIGRETTE or try grating the ZEST on to hot buttered PASTA.

Lentils are a pulse vegetable and therefore very important in a vegetarian diet. They're used a lot in Indian and Eastern cookery (see INDIAN VEGETARIAN FOOD). There are three well-known kinds:
- split red lentils (tiny and bright orange)
- whole green lentils (quite large and greenish)
- continental or brown lentils (yes, you've guessed, they're brown!)

Lettuce is commonly listed as a SALAD ingredient. There are quite a few different sorts, such as Cos, Little Gem, Lollo Rosso (purple-green and frilly), Iceberg (very crispy), and they all have different tastes. Try them for yourself.

...lettuce....

Limes can be used in much the same way as LEMONS. Again, experiment.

Litchi (also spelt lichee and lichi) is a small fruit which originated in China. Its brittle pinkish coloured skin protects a white pulp and a relatively large stone. You only eat the pulp. Litchi can be bought in tins, but they taste nothing like the fresh fruit, which are available in good greengrocers' and large supermarkets.

...litchi....

Maize is also known as CORN.

Meat is avoided by vegetarians for many reasons:
- Some vegetarians believe that it's cruel to kill ANIMALS, birds and fish for food.
- Some vegetarians are concerned about eating animals for health reasons. For instance, they don't like the fact that many animals are given hormones to encourage growth, and that these remain in the meat people buy.
- Some vegetarians find FACTORY FARMING totally unacceptable.
- Some vegetarians believe that eating meat is very unfair to the people in the world who are starving. Over 50 per cent of the world's total cereal crop is fed to animals which are then killed to provide meat. For instance, in 1984–5 GRAIN was imported from Ethiopia into Britain to feed cattle. Ethiopia was suffering severe famine at the time. Meat is an expensive way of providing food and it's the poor of the world who pay by suffering malnutrition (malnutrition is the term given to someone who has had a very poor DIET for a long time). It's

thought that 30,000 people die *every day* from malnutrition. If grain, which is at present fed to animals eaten by people who live in relatively wealthy countries, was used instead to feed human beings, this would be a major step towards preventing starvation in poorer countries.

● Some vegetarians are very concerned about rainforests. (See JUNK FOOD.)

Milk and milk products are useful in vegetarian cooking. There are a number of different types:

● skimmed milk has had most of the fat which is naturally present removed. It's richer in calcium than ordinary milk;

● buttermilk is the leftover liquid from butter-making;

● cream is the fat part of milk;

- cream CHEESE is made from unskimmed milk and cream;
- pasteurized milk and cream are heat-treated to help them last longer;
- curds and whey are the solid and liquid left when milk separates;
- YOGHURT.

Some vegetarians and all VEGANS choose not to drink or eat milk or milk products. Many use SOYA milk instead.

Millet is a nutritious cereal rich in iron and quick to cook. It can be used instead of RICE in many dishes. Try it and see what you think.

Minerals which are present in the soil and the sea are inorganic, so you can't eat them. Plants can absorb minerals into their cell structure and it's via plants that you get your necessary intake. They are vital to prevent disease, but you don't need to worry about them too much if you're eating a well-balanced DIET. (You don't, for instance, need to take mineral pills such as iron tablets unless your doctor tells you to.) But it's still good to have an idea of what's in what, so here are some of the most important minerals and some of the main vegetarian foods in which they are found:

- Calcium – MILK, CHEESE, MILLET, sesame SEEDS, NUTS
- Copper – cereals, DRIED FRUITS, green vegetables
- Iron – EGGS (yolk), LENTILS, BEANS, GRAINS, YEAST
- Potassium – prunes, GRAINS, NUTS, bananas, WHEATGERM
- Magnesium – green cabbage, NUTS, SOYA BEANS
- Zinc – EGGS, YEAST, wholemeal BREAD sunflower SEEDS

Molasses is a sticky, almost black syrup. It's the leftover product after cane sugar has been refined. Used as a sweetener, you'll come across it in recipes for teabreads and cakes. Its rich in the MINERAL iron and VITAMIN C.

mushrooms

Mushrooms are edible fungi and a brilliant substitute for meat. There are many varieties, but the two main types are:

- button – nice raw in salads or dips, but they're good for cooking too. Try frying slices in butter or margarine and parsley. Serve on hot toast for a snack or cooked breakfast.
- flat-cap – have quite a strong flavour. They're great stuffed (see below) or to make stuffing with and can be used to add flavour to all sorts of dishes.

(See also GOULASH, RAGOUT, RICE-*RISOTTO*, STROGANOFF, XMAS NUT BAKE.)

recipe

Mushrooms Stuffed with Herbs (for 2)
This is an easy dish to make, but it looks really special. Make sure you share it with someone – they'll be impressed!

4 large flat-capped MUSHROOMS, washed, dried and peeled
25 g (1 oz) butter
100 g (4 oz) cream cheese
1 dessertspoon fresh HERBS (chives and parsley are good), washed and chopped
1 clove GARLIC, peeled and crushed
2 cherry tomatoes, washed and cut in half
25 g (1 oz) CHEESE, grated

1) Remove the stalks from the mushrooms and chop them finely, leaving the caps whole.
2) Heat the butter in a large frying pan and add the mushroom caps. Cook for 3–4 minutes (until mushrooms are slightly soft).
3) Remove mushrooms from pan and dry them with kitchen paper.
4) In a bowl, mix the cream cheese, herbs, garlic and mushroom stalks.
5) Stuff a quarter of the mixture into each mushroom cap.
6) Press half a tomato (cut side up) into the middle of each filled mushroom.
7) Sprinkle a little grated cheese on top of each mushroom.
8) Put the mushrooms into a flameproof dish and cook them under a very hot grill until the cheese bubbles.
9) Serve immediately with crusty BREAD and a SALAD in summer or a JACKET POTATO and STIR-FRIED vegetables in winter.

Mustard is a plant the seeds of which are crushed into a powder and used to make a paste which is served with food or used in cooking, e.g. to add extra flavour to a CHEESE sauce or VINAIGRETTE.

Noodles are made from a flour and EGG dough. They are usually bought in dried form and used in soups and Chinese cooking.

Nutrition. Nutritious food is healthy and good for you. Good nutrition means a healthy DIET and whatever MEAT eaters might tell you, vegetarians can have very healthy diets. But, you have to know what you're eating and make sure that you're having the right sorts of things. This means you must eat certain foods regularly to get all the VITAMINS, fat, PROTEIN, carbohydrates, and MINERALS that your body needs. Every day you should try to eat:

- some foods which are rich in protein (EGGS, CHEESE, YOGHURT, MILK, NUTS, PULSES, SEEDS). It's no good only drinking milk, because you need the mixture of different kinds of protein which is supplied by these different foods;
- some foods which are rich in carbohydrates (e.g. brown RICE, brown BREAD, GRAINS, wholemeal PASTA);
- some fresh green vegetables which contain important MINERALS (e.g. cabbage, broccoli and SPINACH);
- some fresh fruit.

Also, get into the habit of eating DRIED FRUIT, such as apricots, as a snack instead of crisps and sweets.

Nuts are a good source of PROTEIN and MINERALS (such as iron and zinc) in a vegetarian DIET. They can be eaten as a healthy snack or combined with vegetables or GRAINS as part of a nutritious main meal. Nuts have distinctive flavours and they're used in a variety of ways – here are a few to try out:

- Almonds – their essence is used for flavouring puddings and sweets. Finely ground, almonds are the main ingredient in marzipan. Ground almonds can also be used to make a rich PASTRY or mixed with breadcrumbs for a savoury crust. You can buy almonds whole, shelled, ground, flaked or chopped for general use in cooking. They're also delicious freshly cracked and eaten as a snack.
- Brazils are great eaten with chocolate.
- Cashews have a sweet flavour and are rather expensive. They're used in curry and in some Chinese dishes.
- Chestnuts, roasted on hot coals, are traditionally sold from street stalls in London around Christmas time. But they can be eaten in lots of other ways. Look out for tins of sweetened chestnut purée – yummy dished up with a blob of thick cream.
- Hazelnuts are good in XMAS nut bakes and nut cookies. Try toasting shelled hazelnuts under a grill (watch carefully and shake occasionally). Delicious!
- Macadamias are mainly imported from Malawi in Africa. They're delicious but expensive and so tend not to be used very often in cooking.
- Peanuts must be the most famous nut – after all, no other nut has a cartoon strip named after it! Peanut butter on hunks of BREAD is a good vegetarian snack. It's pretty good spooned straight from the jar too! Peanuts are used a great deal in

···nuts··· ···nuts···

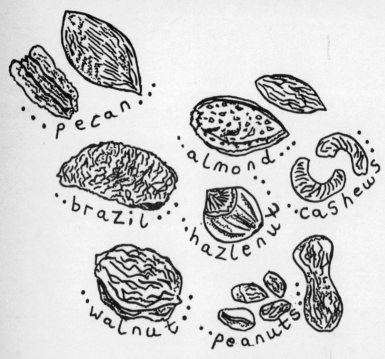

pecan

almond

brazil

hazlenut

cashews

walnut

peanuts

Eastern cookery (for instance in Indonesian satay sauce) and African cookery.

- Pecans are very popular in America, where they're grown in huge numbers. Try pecan pie when you get the chance – it's incredibly filling!

- Walnuts are pressed to make walnut OIL which is popular in France and can be used for a really tasty VINAIGRETTE. In Britain walnut pieces are often used to decorate coffee-flavoured cakes or pressed into soft CHEESES.

Nut Burgers (for 3–4)

These crunchy nut burgers tend to fall apart a bit as you fry them. Don't worry – they'll still taste good and a big squirt of tomato ketchup will hide the broken bits. You can eat them with chips, vegetables, SALAD, YAM MASH, or try them in a roll with some fried onions and mustard – better than a hot dog!

25 g (1 oz) butter
1 onion, chopped
100 g (4 oz) BREAD made into crumbs in a BLENDER
225 g (8 oz) mixed NUTS (buy them pre-chopped)
1 free-range EGG lightly beaten
2 teaspoons YEAST EXTRACT mixed with 2 tablespoons boiling WATER
OIL for frying

1) Melt the butter in a medium saucepan.
2) Fry the onion until golden brown.
3) Turn off the heat and add the breadcrumbs, nuts, egg and yeast extract. Add salt and pepper if you wish. Mix well.
4) Divide the nut mixture into eight to ten equal portions.
5) Use your hands to press each portion into a burger shape.
6) Fry the burgers in hot oil for about four minutes on each side (they should be golden brown).
7) Eat hot or cold.

Oat is a GRAIN rich in protein, VITAMIN B and iron, and it's not only used for porridge! For tastier PASTRY and crumble toppings, replace some of the flour with oatflakes.

In Scotland oatcakes (thin dry biscuits) are eaten with butter or CHEESE, but they taste good with peanut butter or jam too.

...recipe...

Oat and Golden Syrup Slices (10 pieces)
Forget bought BISCUITS – these are the real thing!

100 g (4 oz) butter
90 g (3½ oz) brown sugar

1 tablespoon golden syrup
170 g (6 oz) rolled OATS
½ teaspoon ground ginger
40 g (1½ oz) mixed NUTS, chopped

1) Grease a 15 cm-square tin and set the oven to 180°C/350°F/Gas Mark 4.
2) Heat the butter in a medium saucepan.
3) Add the sugar and golden syrup and keep heating gently until they melt. Stir all the time.
4) Turn off the heat.
5) Add the oats, ginger and nuts. Stir well. The mixture should be really thick and gungy.
6) Tip the mixture into the greased tin and press down firmly. Use the back of a wooden spoon to make it really flat.
7) Bake for 20–30 minutes till golden brown.
8) Remove from the oven and mark into squares with a blunt knife. Cool in tin.
9) When cold, store in an airtight container.

Oil contains VITAMINS
A, D, E and K. There are quite
a few different types of oil
which each have different flavours.
Here are some to try out:

- olive – use to shallow fry and in a VINAIGRETTE
- walnut – use in a vinaigrette
- sesame – use in a vinaigrette
- rapeseed – use in a vinaigrette
- sunflower – use for general frying
- soya – use for general frying
- corn – use for general frying

Okra (also known as 'lady's finger'!) is a small, pointed, green vegetable with a ridged skin. It originated in Africa and is now popular in African and West Indian cookery. Try it in a VEGETABLE CURRY.

Olives are a fruit picked while unripe and then pickled. If you've tried olives and don't like them, give them a second chance on top of pizza or PASTA because their taste does vary depending on their colour, size and how they have been pickled.

Organic farming means not using chemicals, such as PESTI-CIDES. Organic farmers use natural fertilizers on their land. They also change the crops which they grow each year, which is a natural way of reducing the numbers of pests. This is known as crop rotation. It's also good because it gives the soil a chance to recover. Some crops, such as clover, actually improve the soil. Organic farming costs more than intensive farming with chemicals, and that means organic food is more expensive to buy, but the more we buy, the cheaper and the more widely available it will become.

Packed lunch (See SANDWICHES)

Pasta is enjoyed by many MEAT eaters, who often combine it with bits of animal to make a meal. Vegetarians prefer to eat pasta combined with vegetables – it tastes even better this way (who's biased?). Pasta comes in many different kinds and shapes; here are a few:

- cannelloni – tubes of pasta sometimes stuffed with meat, but often with a tasty spinach filling
- conchiglie – shell-shaped pieces of pasta
- lasagna – sheets of pasta, layered between savoury sauces which are often meaty, though vegetable alternatives are now widely available
- ravioli – little pillows of pasta with tasty fillings (make sure you get a vegetarian filling, not meat)
- spaghetti – skinny strands of pasta
- tagliatelle – skinny flat ribbons of pasta

All types of pasta are easy to cook. Just fill a large pan with plenty of water and bring it to the boil. Pour in a little cooking oil (the cheat's way to stop pasta sticking together!), then tip in the pasta.

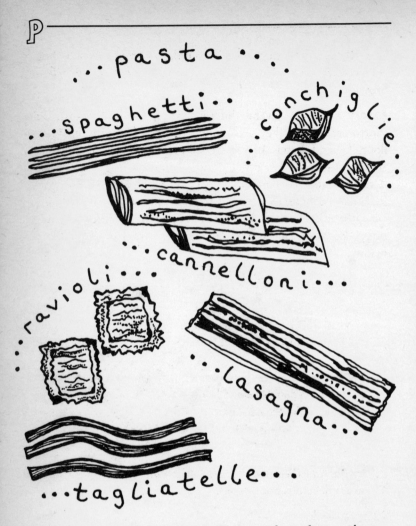

...pasta...
...spaghetti...
...conchiglie...
...cannelloni...
...ravioli...
...lasagna...
...tagliatelle...

Boil until the pasta is cooked (2–20 minutes depending on the type of pasta and its thickness, so keep testing it).

To make a simple pasta sauce, mash a ripe avocado (soft but not squishy) until it forms a paste. Mix in a small tub of natural

YOGHURT, until the sauce is completely green. Add to hot or cold cooked pasta. Eat it quickly, or your green sauce will turn brown!

Pastry comes in several different types, the best known being shortcrust, puff, flakey and choux. Pastry is basically made from flour, fat and water. It doesn't look as if it contains any bits of animal, but sometimes it does. Lard, dripping or suet, which are all ANIMAL fats, are sometimes used in ready-prepared pastry, and EGGS are sometimes added for a richer flavour. That's OK if you eat eggs, but you still have no way of knowing whether they're free range. So read labels carefully or make your own pastry (see below).

..recipe...

Pastry Purses Filled with Curried Vegetables (for 4)
These are delicious hot or cold.

225 g (8 oz) flour
100 g (4 oz) margarine, cut into little pieces
cold WATER
1 tablespoon OIL
1 onion, chopped

1 teaspoon curry powder
1 carrot, scrubbed and chopped into 1 cm chunks
1 potato, peeled and chopped into 1 cm chunks
1 parsnip, peeled and chopped into 1 cm chunks
a little MILK

First, make the shortcrust pastry:

1) Sift the flour into a large bowl.
2) Add the margarine.
3) Rub the margarine into the flour. You do this by picking up some flour and margarine with your fingertips and then rubbing them together about 20 cm above the bowl so that as the flour and margarine fall they trap air, which will make the pastry light. (It isn't nearly as difficult to do as it sounds!)
4) Stop rubbing when the flour and margarine mix looks like breadcrumbs.
5) Add 3–4 tablespoons of water.
6) Mix together with a blunt knife.
7) Everything should stick together to make a smooth dough. If it's too wet and sticky add a little more flour – if it's too dry add a little more water.
8) Wrap the pastry in foil and leave it in the fridge while you make the vegetable filling.

To make the curried vegetable filling:

1) Heat the oil in a medium sized saucepan. Add the onion and fry gently for 5 minutes.
2) Add the curry powder and stir well.
3) Add the other vegetables and stir well.
4) Put a lid on the saucepan and cook gently for about 15 minutes (give it a quick stir about once every 5 minutes to make sure that none of the vegetables have stuck to the bottom of the pan).

5) Remove the pan from the heat. Tip the vegetables into a dish and leave them to cool.

To make the purses:

1) Cut the pastry dough into four equal portions.
2) Sprinkle some flour on to the work surface and on to a rolling pin.
3) Roll out each pastry portion into a circle (it doesn't have to be a perfect circle!).
4) Put a quarter of the vegetable filling into the centre of each circle.
5) Wet the edge of the circle with a little water.
6) Gather the pastry edges together around the filling, and pinch them to form a pastry purse. Cut off any messy bits with a sharp knife.
7) Brush the purses with a little milk.
8) With a sharp knife, cut a small slit in each purse.
9) Place the purses on a greased baking tray and put them into the oven, preheated to 190°C/375°F/Gas Mark 5.
10) Bake until golden brown.

Pâté has traditionally been made from MEAT, but very tasty vegetable pâtés are now available in the shops.

Pearl barley is the rounded grains of BARLEY with the outer husks removed. It can be added to vegetable stews or soups.

Peppers (also known as capsicum) can be eaten raw or cooked. They come in three different colours:
- green (unripe)
- red (ripe)
- yellow (ripe)

(See CHILLI SIN CARNE, GOULASH, VEGETABLE CURRY.)

Pesticides are sprayed on to crops to kill off pests. However, they can also kill butterflies and ladybirds. They quite often harm small animals too and can end up in the food we eat. (See ORGANIC FARMING.)

Plantain is the fruit of a tropical plant and it looks very much like a large banana except that it's green. It is popular in West Indian cookery.

Pomegranates are the fruit of a tropical tree which grows in North Africa and Western Asia. The tough reddish skin protects hundreds of pulpy seeds which are the edible part of the fruit.

Pomelo is a sort of grapefruit.

Protein is vital for a healthy DIET. MEAT contains a lot of protein and many meat eaters use this as an excuse for not becoming vegetarian. However, it's perfectly possible to get plenty of protein without having to eat a single mouthful of animal flesh. Good non-meat sources of protein are EGGS, YOGHURT, MILK, and CHEESE. If you eat some of these regularly along with NUTS, GRAINS and PULSES, you'll easily be getting enough protein. (Doctors sometimes advise people to eat other foods too, and if this happens to you it is important to stick to what the doctor says.)

Pulse is the name given to a group of foods consisting of BEANS, peas and LENTILS. They are important sources of PROTEIN and therefore form quite a large part of many vegetarian's DIETS. Pulses have been eaten for a long time – it's possible that Egyptian cooks used them over 2,000 years ago. You can buy pulses in dried form, frozen (peas), or in tins. If you use tinned pulses, e.g. BEANS, they will have been cooked already and all you have to do is drain them and add them to the other ingredients you're using. Dried pulses must be soaked and then boiled well. It's *very* important that you do so as some pulses are poisonous if they are not boiled for long enough.

Questions and answers. If you're a new vegetarian or want to become one there are probably lots of questions you'd like answered – here are a few of the most common:

Q I really want to be a vegetarian but I love bacon. How can I give it up?
A Willpower! Though you can give your willpower a hand by calling what's on your plate pig instead of bacon. Then imagine a labrador chained up in a tiny stall and unable to turn around, and remember that a pig is probably at least as intelligent as a dog. Do you *really* still want to eat bacon? (See TOFU.)

Q My parents won't let me become a vegetarian, so what can I do?
A If your parents refuse to let you become a vegetarian, then there's not much you can do about it when you eat at home. However, perhaps they're just concerned that you might not eat well and have a healthy DIET. If so, the best thing to do is to learn as much as you can about NUTRITION and show them that you intend to eat plenty of good food. Outside your home you can exercise more choice: say no to burgers and other FAST FOOD;

76

ask for vegetarian food at school/college; tell friends that, if possible, you prefer vegetarian food.

Q Everyone else in my family eats meat, and I just have to eat what I'm given. I can't not eat, can I?

A No, you can't not eat. But you can offer to cook a vegetarian meal for your family. If your parents have been meat eaters all their lives they probably don't know how to cook vegetarian meals, so it's up to you to show them that a veggy dish can be healthy, cheap, quick to cook and very tasty. You can also exercise choice outside your home – saying no to FAST FOOD is a big step in the right direction.

Q Does a vegetarian eat fish?

A No. However, many people start by not eating pigs, cows, chickens and sheep. Then, when they've learned to cook vegetarian dishes/convinced their parents/etc., they stop eating fish too.

Vegetarians are often asked awkward questions by friends and family, too. So here are a few of the most common questions along with a few good replies:

Q What would happen if we all stopped eating meat?

A First of all, people won't all stop eating animals overnight, however much we might want them to. The change from meat eating to vegetarianism would be gradual. So, as the demand for lamb chops and pork sausages, fried bacon and roast chicken, smoked salmon and prawn cocktails, minced beef and doner KEBABS, drops, so the number of pigs, cows, sheep and chickens farmed (and particularly FACTORY FARMed) will drop. We won't suddenly have fields (or battery farms) full of animals which no one wants, rather as demand falls farmers will breed fewer animals for slaughter.

Q Isn't vegetarian food really, really, boring – all that rabbit food?
A Vegetarian food is far from boring! For a start it's got loads of colour (you can actually see the colour of your food when it isn't smothered in dark brown gravy), and it usually has more variety too. If anything it's 'meat and two veg' which is boring. If anyone calls your choice of DIET 'rabbit food', then they're just being rude – don't let them get to you.

Q Mmm . . . err . . . don't vegetarians have a lot of umm . . . wind?
A Tricky one, this. Yes, parts of a vegetarian diet *do* create more than their fair share of wind (OK, farts!) but you probably won't be eating that much of them or that often. Anyway, so what? If you're worried, read the section on MEAT again and decide for yourself where your priorities lie.

Q Aren't you a hypocrite because you still wear leather shoes/belts/bags/jackets?
A Yes! But it's better to start somewhere than never to start at all. This means that if you've been brought up in a meat-eating family where it's OK to wear leather boots/jackets/shoes/etc., then changing to a vegetarian diet is harder than if you've been brought up in a 'right on' family. So, if you've changed to vegetarian food but still wear leather shoes, give yourself a pat on the back for making a start and promise yourself to try even harder. It's only fashion that dictates that leather looks good. After all, no one thinks fur's fun any more. Your parents may insist that leather's best for your feet (though trainers are good too) but they're not likely to insist that you must have an expensive leather coat/belt/bag. The choice is yours and, frankly, it's not hard to make the right decision.

Q You don't think that you're going to make a difference to anything, do you?

A Yes! It's the simple law of supply and demand. If you demand free-range EGGS, then they will become available; if you say no to FAST FOOD, outlets will eventually close; if you demand vegetarian products such as TOFU and QUORN, then shops will sell them; if you show friends and family that vegetarian food is fun, then they might be tempted to try some; if you say no to leather belts, bags, etc., other fabrics will become fashionable. The power for change is with *you*.

...recipe...

Quiche (for 4)

This recipe is for a spring onion quiche, but you can experiment with other fillings such as tomato or sweetcorn.

170 g (6 oz) shortcrust PASTRY (for method see page 72)
2 free-range EGGS
6 spring onions, washed, dried and chopped
125 ml (¼ pint) MILK
100 g (4 oz) Cheddar CHEESE, grated

1) Turn the oven on to 170°C/325°F/Gas Mark 3.
2) Roll out the pastry and use it to line a 20 cm (8 inch) greased quiche dish.
3) Prick the pastry all over with a fork.
4) Bake for 25 minutes.
5) While the pastry case is cooking, mix together the eggs, spring onions, milk and 50 g (2 oz) of the cheese.

6) When the pastry has turned pale brown, take it out of the oven.
7) Pour in the filling mixture and sprinkle the extra cheese on the top.
8) Return the quiche to the oven and bake until the filling puffs up and turns golden brown.
9) Eat the quiche either warm or cold. It's good with a GREEN SALAD.

Quince is a very hard fruit which originated in Japan. It makes delicious quince jelly (try it in a sandwich with peanut butter).

Quorn is a fairly new product to hit the supermarket shelves. It's made from a MUSHROOM-like plant and is a useful vegetarian convenience food for anyone who is used to eating chunks of meat. Quorn comes in cubes and has a texture which is something like lamb or chicken.

..quorn..

Ragoût is traditionally a meat stew, but you can adapt recipes by using mushrooms instead of meat and vegetable STOCK instead of meat stock.

Relish, or chutney, is a bit like ketchup and can be served with the same sorts of food, e.g. chips. Look out for relishes such as cucumber, mango and tomato in delicatessens and large supermarkets. They're really good with curry (See INDIAN VEGETARIAN FOOD) and with dishes made from NUTS.

Rennet is something you'll never want to eat again, once you know what it is. Rennet is the curdled MILK found in the stomach of a very young calf. It's also the term given to the part of the stomach membrane which is used to curdle milk and make it into CHEESE or JUNKET. Occasionally you might come across rennet made from plant membrane, but this is rare, so check it out carefully.

Rice is a GRAIN. It comes in two main colours – brown (unprocessed, and therefore healthier) and white (processed) and in two main types – long grain and short grain. White rice can cook in about 10 minutes, but brown rice can take up to 25 minutes, so follow the instructions on the packet. You can serve cooked rice plain or you can make it more interesting by adding:

- a knob of butter
- LEMON juice and ZEST
- chopped DRIED FRUIT
- chopped NUTS (See INDIAN VEGETARIAN FOOD)
- chopped HERBS (try fresh coriander)
- marigold petals (washed and carefully dried)
- chopped fresh fruit
- olive OIL and chopped GARLIC
- chopped hardboiled EGGS (See KEDGEREE)
- chopped OLIVES
- cooked peas
- chopped MUSHROOMS (See RISOTTO below)
- grated coconut

...rice...

Rice cakes look like polystyrene. Do they taste like it too? Try them and see.

Rye is a cereal used in Northern European countries to make bread.

Radish and Cucumber Salad (for 4)

½ cucumber, washed, dried and thinly sliced
8 large radishes, washed, 'tops and tails' removed and thinly sliced
2 tablespoons VINAIGRETTE

1) Arrange the cucumber and radishes on four small plates.
2) Sprinkle with vinaigrette.
3) Serve with RYE BREAD.

Risotto (for 4)

Risotto is an Italian dish which is made with RICE, STOCK and usually meat. In this recipe MUSHROOMS have been used instead of meat.

1 tablespoon cooking OIL
450 g (1 lb) MUSHROOMS, washed and chopped
1 clove GARLIC crushed
225 g (8 oz) RICE (brown or white)
500 ml (1 pint) vegetable STOCK
25 g (1 oz) butter
50 g (2 oz) finely grated CHEESE (Parmesan tastes best)
bunch of fresh parsley, chopped

1) Heat the cooking oil in a large frying pan and add the mushrooms and garlic. Cook for five minutes, stirring from time-to-time.
2) Add the rice and stir until it's coated with oil.
3) Add the vegetable stock gradually.

4) Cook gently until all the stock has disappeared and the rice is soft (about 30–40 minutes).
5) Mix in the grated cheese, butter, parsley and pepper to taste.
6) Serve hot.

Rhubarb and Gingernut Cream (for 4)

675 g (1½ lb) rhubarb, washed and cut into 2 cm pieces
75 g (3 oz) sugar
250 ml (½ pint) double cream
8 gingernut BISCUITS, broken into pieces (but not crumbs)

1) Put the rhubarb and sugar into a saucepan. Add enough WATER to just cover the bottom of the pan.
2) Put a lid on the pan and cook gently until the rhubarb breaks down into a messy looking mush (keep checking to make sure that the rhubarb doesn't stick to the bottom – you may have to add a little more water).
3) Tip the cooked rhubarb into a bowl and leave it to go cold.
4) Add the cream and stir well.
5) Stir in the gingernuts just before serving.

Salad is a dish made from a combination of cold foods. A wide range of ingredients can be used in a salad including vegetables (cooked or raw), cooked PULSES, FRUIT, GRAINS and NUTS. Salads are good as part of a balanced DIET because they are high in FIBRE, and when freshly prepared with raw fruit and vegetables they are particularly high in VITAMINS.

Sandwiches don't always have to be filled with CHEESE if you're a vegetarian! Here are some ideas for other fillings, which can be

used with any sort of bread:

- ALFALFA and HUMMUS
- BEAN SPROUTS and TAHINI
- DRIED FRUIT and cream cheese
- grated carrot mixed with mayonnaise and slices of hardboiled EGG
- sliced tomatoes and HUMMUS
- NUT pâté (from large supermarkets) and lettuce
- cottage cheese and chopped red PEPPER
- cream cheese and HONEY
- cucumber, butter BEANS (cold, cooked) and mayonnaise
- mashed hardboiled egg and mayonnaise
- mashed cold cooked butter beans with olive OIL and LEMON ZEST
- mashed cold cooked chick peas with mayonnaise and curry powder
- mashed cold cooked kidney beans with a little butter and CHILLI powder
- chopped or grated nuts with cream CHEESE
- chocolate and nut spread (2 tablespoons golden syrup, 1 tablespoon cocoa powder, 25 g (1 oz) soft margarine and 1 dessertspoon chopped nuts)

Sauerkraut is a German dish of pickled white cabbage. It's sold in jars in many supermarkets. Try serving it with CHEESE-filled JACKET POTATOES or veggie burgers.

Sauté is a term you will often come across in cookery books. If you're told to sauté the vegetables it means that you should heat some OIL in a pan and fry them for 2–3 minutes, stirring all the time.

Seaweed is very NUTRITIOUS and it's delicious – try it and see for yourself. Dried seaweed is sold in Chinese supermarkets and health stores. Look for carrageen, dulse, nori or AGAR-AGAR. To cook it, simply heat a little OIL and toss the dried seaweed in it until it's hot, glossy and crisp. Flavour with a little salt and serve with NOODLES and STIR-FRIED vegetables.

...seaweed...

Seeds have all sorts of uses in cooking. Here are some which are fairly easily available:
- sesame seeds are the tiny seeds which, when crushed, are used to make the paste TAHINI;
- pumpkin seeds are the 'biggies', and are rich in the MINERAL zinc;
- caraway seeds may be used to flavour BREAD, cake and sometimes VINAIGRETTE;
- poppy seeds have a delicate flavour and are used to make a tasty topping for BREAD.

Soya is an incredibly useful PULSE. It's packed with PROTEIN and is used to make substitutes for dairy products, such as soya MILK. It's also used to make soya flour, TSP and TOFU.

Spinach made Popeye strong. Why? Because the cartoon maker said so! However, spinach is a very healthy food with lots of VITAMINS and MINERALS.

Stir-fried means food fried lightly (often in a wok) and stirred all the time. Vegetables cook quickly like this, and they stay crisp.

Stock in many recipe books refers to a liquid made from WATER, HERBS and MEAT. It's used in cooking as it has more flavour than water alone. You can make your own vegetable stock, but it takes quite a bit of effort. So, unless you're a really keen cook, cheat with a vegetable stock cube.

Suet is the hard fat which covers the kidneys of sheep and oxen. It's an ingredient of mincemeat and Christmas puddings, so use the vegetarian version now widely available in supermarkets.

Stroganoff (for 2)
Stroganoff is a Russian dish which is usually made with strips of

meat and sour cream. This easy recipe uses MUSHROOMS instead of steak.

40 g (1½ oz) butter
450 g (1 lb) mushrooms, washed, dried and sliced
125 ml (¼ pint) sour cream
½ teaspoon grated nutmeg

1) Melt the butter in a medium saucepan.
2) Add the mushrooms, STIR-FRY for 5 minutes and remove from heat.
3) Add the sour cream and heat gently for 1 minute (do not boil).
4) Add salt and pepper if you want to.
5) Serve with boiled RICE and decorate with nutmeg.

Sweetcorn, known as CORN or MAIZE in America, is a useful ingredient for salads and stews. It can be bought fresh (on the cob), frozen or canned. It's an ingredient in Mexican TORTILLAS.

corn on the cob.. (sweet corn)

Tahini is something you'll either love or loathe! It's a paste made from sesame SEEDS and it tends to stick to the roof of your mouth, but apart from that it's pretty good! Try eating it with CRUDITÉS.

Take-aways (See FAST FOODS.)

Taman is a fermented soya sauce.

Tempura is a dish which comes from Japan, where it was traditionally made with small pieces of fish coated in batter and deep fried. Vegetable tempura is now more widely available and it's delicious – try it if you get the chance.

Terrine is a term used in cookery to mean something which has been made, or which is being served, in a pottery container.

Tofu is used quite a lot in Japanese cookery. It's made from

ground SOYA BEANS. As it tastes fairly bland, tofu takes on the flavours of the foods you cook with it. Try cutting it into 2 cm squares and adding it to STIR-FRIED vegetables.

...recipe...

Tofu Salad (for 4)

New vegetarians tend to miss the taste of smoked bacon. Well, smoked tofu has the same smokey flavour and smell. Crispy fried bacon bits are sometimes used in meat cookery to add smokey flavour and crunch to salad. This recipe uses smoked tofu instead of bacon, but as tofu is soft you have to use a really crisp salad vegetable, such as CHICORY or BEAN SPROUTS, to add crunch.

4 tablespoons cooking OIL
225 g (8 oz) packet smoked tofu, drained and cut into small blocks
2 heads of chicory washed, dried and finely shredded
4 SPINACH leaves, washed, dried and finely shredded
225 g (8 oz) bean sprouts, washed and dried
4 tablespoons VINAIGRETTE.

1) Heat the oil in a large frying pan.
2) Add the tofu and fry until pale golden brown.
3) Turn off the heat and carefully remove the tofu pieces from the

pan (they may break up a bit, but that doesn't matter), then put them on to a plate to cool.

4) Put the chicory, spinach and bean sprouts into a large salad bowl and add vinaigrette. Mix well.
5) Put the pieces of tofu on top of the salad.
6) Serve with French BREAD.

Tortilla is a flat 'cake' made from MAIZE. It's very popular in South America, where it's eaten hot wrapped around all sorts of delicious fillings. You can buy tortillas in packets in large supermarkets – why not invent your own filling for them?

...tortilla...

Tossed salad is a salad which has been well coated in VINAI-GRETTE. That's all!

TSP stands for Textured Soya Protein. It's a product made from SOYA BEANS and can be used instead of minced meat.

Ugli is a sort of cross between a grapefruit, an orange and a tangerine. It's a mottled yellow and green colour and gets its name from its wrinkly skin. Uglis come from the West Indies.

ugli fruit

...recipe...

Ugli Fruit Muesli (for 1)

Muesli's good for you but it can also be pretty boring after a while, so, try it this way for a change.

1 ugli, peeled
1 bowl muesli
1 teaspoon HONEY (more if you've got a sweet tooth!)
2 tablespoons YOGHURT

1) Cut the flesh of the ugli into chunks. Add it to the muesli.
2) Add the honey and yoghurt and mix well.
3) Eat it!

Unrefined foods are those which haven't been over-processed. When food is refined, much of its NUTRITIONAL value is lost. For example, white flour (used in most cakes, biscuits, PASTRY and white BREAD) has had most of its VITAMINS, MINERALS and FIBRE removed along with its outer brown husk. So whenever you can, choose foods which are unrefined (such as brown bread, RICE and PASTA).

Veal is the flesh of a calf. (See FACTORY FARMING.)

Vegan is the name given to a strict vegetarian who eats no animals and no animal products. So, unlike vegetarians, vegans don't eat EGGS, CHEESE, MILK, butter or YOGHURT. A vegan diet can be excellent. However, you really must understand about NUTRITION before you change to a completely vegan lifestyle. If you want to become a vegan, it's a good idea to do so gradually. First, become a vegetarian (which means that you will still eat eggs, cheese, milk and yoghurt, but not MEAT, birds or fish). Take plenty of time (probably several years) to learn how to cook lots of vegan dishes using ingredients such as GRAINS, PULSES and TOFU. Learn about the nutritional requirements for a healthy DIET. Then, when you're an experienced vegetarian, you can gradually stop eating all animal products.

...vegan...
...fruit... ...vegetables...
...beans...

..recipe...

Vegetable Curry (for 4)
Serve this tasty curry with RICE and a side dish of cucumber raita.

Curry
1 large potato
2 ZUCCHINI
3 tomatoes
3 carrots
½ green PEPPER
½ red pepper
1 large onion
a little cooking OIL
4 teaspoons curry powder
1 dessertspoon apricot jam
125 ml (¼ pint) MILK
250 ml (½ pint) vegetable STOCK or WATER

1) Wash and finely chop the vegetables.
2) Fry the onion in oil until soft.
3) Add the curry powder and the jam and mix together well.
4) Add the milk and stir to make a paste.
5) Add the remaining vegetables and stir well.
6) Add the stock or water and bring to the boil, then reduce the heat and simmer gently for about 50 minutes.

Cucumber Raita
1 small tub YOGHURT
10 cm chunk of cucumber
paprika

1) Chop the cucumber into thin strips.
2) Mix with the yoghurt.
3) Decorate with a sprinkle of paprika.

Vinaigrette is a kind of salad dressing. It's made from mixing OIL and VINEGAR with various flavourings. To make your own vinaigrette, put two tablespoons of olive oil and two tablespoons of wine vinegar into a jar. Screw the lid on tightly and shake well. That's all there is to it! To make the vinaigrette special, try adding:

- ½ teaspoon grainy MUSTARD and ½ teaspoon HONEY
- chopped clove of GARLIC
- ZEST of a LEMON
- chopped fresh HERBS
- a little brown sugar
- teaspoon soy sauce

...vinaigrette...

V

Vinegar is a very sour-tasting liquid which is made from wine, cider or malt. It's most often used in cookery to make a VINAIGRETTE.

Vitamins are necessary for a healthy DIET, but you don't have to worry about them much if you're a vegetarian because they're present in plants. So, unless a doctor tells you to, there's no need for you to take vitamin pills.

Vol-au-vent is a French word which translates (roughly) as 'light as air'. Vol-au-vents are small cases made from puff PASTRY and filled with a sauce. They're pretty unfashionable at the moment, but that's a pity because they taste and look good. You can buy frozen vol-au-vent cases and fill them with whatever you want.

Waffles are a type of pancake made from a batter. Plastered with maple syrup, they're popular at breakfast time in America, but did you know the name is Dutch (*wafel*) and that they are eaten a lot in Holland and Belgium too?

waffles

Water must rate as the most valuable commodity on the earth, because without water nothing can live. In industrialized countries, we use tap water every day to wash, clean our teeth, cook and drink. However, we also pollute our water supply with chemicals and sewage. Industry is said to cause over a third of all water pollution problems. Waste products from manufacturing are either piped into the sewer system or escape into rivers. AGRICULTURE is another major polluter. Chemical fertilizers and PESTICIDES are washed out of soil and crops by rain and find their way into rivers, lakes and streams and then into reservoirs from which drinking water is pumped. (ORGANIC FARMING does not, of course, use these methods.) Liquid manure (slurry), which farmers spray on to the land, seeps into fresh water and takes oxygen from it. Without oxygen in their water fish die.

..recipe...

Watercress Soup (for 4)
This is a creamy, pale green coloured soup which tastes good hot or cold.

2 tablespoons OIL
1 onion chopped
1 bunch of watercress
750 ml (1½ pints) STOCK
2 slices BREAD, broken into pieces

1) Heat the oil in a large saucepan.
2) Add the onion and fry gently until soft.

3) Add the watercress and stock, and bring to the boil.
4) Put a lid on the pan, then turn the heat down and cook gently for 15 minutes.
5) Turn off the heat and add the bread.
6) Tip the soup into a BLENDER and liquidize for one minute (you may have to do this in two parts if the blender is small).
7) Tip the soup back into the saucepan and reheat.
8) Add salt and pepper if you want to.
9) Serve with any sort of bread.

Whales are killed for meat and for their blubber (fat). Blubber is used to make lots of things including cosmetics. How many people who wear lipstick know that they are smearing bits of whale over their mouths? You're not likely to come across whale meat in the shops, but to avoid cosmetics made with whale choose brands which are known to have been manufactured without cruelty to any animals, such as Beauty Without Cruelty and Body Shop. Whales have been hunted so much that they're now an endangered species. This means that unless humans stop killing them there will soon be none left anywhere in the world. If you feel this is wrong, take some action. Write to your MP and get all your friends and

family to do the same. Tell her/him to take action to save the whale. Here's a sample letter:

Dear [write in the name of your MP – your local library will tell you who it is]

I believe that whales are important and that they should be protected by humans. Please do all you can to stop them being hunted and to stop their oil being used for products such as cosmetics. Could you please write and tell me what action you will take?

Yours sincerely,

[then sign your name]

Send the letter to: The Palace of Westminster, London SW1.

Wheatgerm is rich in Vitamin E and can be sprinkled over your breakfast cereal. It tastes OK, but it's definitely nicer to eat UNREFINED foods instead!

Xmas (OK, so it's a cheat, but there aren't many words which begin with the letter X!) is short for Christmas which, if you're the only vegetarian in your family, can be short for trouble.

In countries where Christmas is celebrated, most family dinners mean MEAT – lots of it. A chicken/turkey/goose is considered by many people to be an essential part of the celebrations. Stuffing the bird with bits of pig (sausage meat) and wrapping it in even more pig (bacon) are all traditional ways of having a good time. Then there's Christmas pud and mince pies which are often made with SUET – more ANIMAL.

Christmas is the time of year when families tend to find plenty of things to argue about, so don't let your vegetarianism become one of them! You could, for instance, create a huge family row by declaring that you won't touch Christmas dinner this year, but there's really no need to be so difficult. Take some time to think about what a typical Christmas Day menu usually includes, and then find ways of adapting it to cause as little trouble as possible.

Here are some tips:

- Suggest that watercress soup (see p. 100) would be good way to start the meal. Arguments to use: it's a great festive green colour; it's cheap and quick to make; it can be served hot or cold; it can be made the day before.

- Remind everyone that you still like carrots, peas and whatever other vegetables are on offer.
- Ask for a few roast potatoes to be cooked in a small tin away from the roast bird.
- Suggest that chestnut rather than sausage meat is used to stuff the bird and ask for some to be cooked in a separate small tin (perhaps with your roast potatoes).
- Point out that an extra helping of cranberry/BREAD/onion sauce will be fine – no need to worry about gravy for you.
- Ask for vegetarian mince pies and Christmas pudding to be bought, or for vegetarian SUET to be used if they're being made at home. Absolutely no one will taste the difference.

If you follow the above tips, the only real problem you'll have is what to do about the main dish, the roast. Most vegetarians declare that they don't mind just having a few more vegetables, but no meat-eating family ever believes them. So you'll have to provide a substitute for the bird. Nut bake is a good idea. It can be made several days before Christmas and kept wrapped in foil in the fridge. It's delicious cold or reheated.

..recipe...

Xmas Nut Bake (8 slices)
1 medium tomato, sliced
25 g (1 oz) sesame SEEDS
40 g (1½ oz) butter
1 large onion, chopped
300 g (12 oz) MUSHROOMS, washed, dried and chopped
1 free-range EGG
250 g (10 oz) white breadcrumbs
1 tablespoon chopped fresh parsley
100 g (4 oz) chopped almonds
50 g (2 oz) ground almonds
100 g (4 oz) no-soak dried apricots, chopped
3 tablespoons vegetable STOCK.

1) Line a 450 g (1 lb) loaf tin with silicon paper. Lay the slices of tomato neatly along the bottom of the lined tin. Sprinkle with the sesame seeds.
2) Heat the butter in a medium saucepan.
3) Add the onion and cook gently until it's pale brown.
4) Add the mushrooms and cook them for about 5 minutes.

5) Tip the onion and mushrooms into a BLENDER and blend for 30 seconds (add a little of the stock if you need to).
6) Pour the thick mushroomy liquid into a large bowl.
7) Add the egg, breadcrumbs, parsley, almonds, apricots and stock. Stir well.
8) Tip the mixture carefully into the loaf tin and press down well using the back of a wooden spoon.
9) Bake at 170°C/325°F/Gas Mark 3 for an hour.
10) Remove from the oven and cool slightly before turning out of the tin and peeling off the paper.
11) Serve in thick slices with dollops of cranberry sauce.

Yam is the edible tuber of a plant which grows in the sub-tropics. Sometimes known as the sweet potato, it's popular in West Indian cookery. Yams can be cooked in the same way as ordinary potatoes.

...yam...
(sweet potato)

...recipe...

Yam Mash (for 2)

450 g (1 lb) yams, peeled and chopped into 2 cm chunks
50 g (2 oz) butter

1) Fill a medium pan with WATER and bring it to the boil.
2) Add the yams and cook until soft (about 20 minutes).
3) Drain off the water.
4) Add the butter and mash well.
5) Add salt and pepper if you wish.
6) Serve with NUT BURGERS.

Yeast has active cells – it's alive! When mixed with water and warmed, yeast gives off a gas. This basic chemistry is used in cooking to make dough for pizza, bread and buns.

Yeast extract is a rich, dark brown paste marketed under various brand names, and produced by mixing brewer's yeast with salt. It's rich in VITAMINS and MINERALS, and good for flavouring stews and casseroles. Nothing beats yeast extract on hot buttered toast!

Yoghurt is made by adding bacteria to milk (usually cow's but also sheep's or goat's) to thicken it. In any supermarket you'll find plain yoghurts plus 'fruit' flavours, which claim to be banana, strawberry, blackcurrant, pineapple, apricot, black cherry, raspberry, etc. – well maybe, but they taste of sugar and are sometimes incredibly lurid colours. Why not make your own? Add fresh fruit (chopped or mashed if necessary) to plain yoghurt (or be inventive, try using prunes, plums, apples, pears or grapes), HONEY is a good sweetener and a few chopped NUTS adds some crunch.

You can use plain yoghurt in other ways:

- Yoghurt can be stirred carefully into soup as a delicious alternative to cream, but make sure that the soup has cooled a little first. If the yoghurt curdles, disguise it with a topping of freshly chopped HERBS.

- Yoghurt salad dressing is very easy to make – flavour plain yoghurt with herbs and/or GARLIC and mix with SALAD ingredients. It doesn't look very good mixed with a green salad so keep to non-leafy ingredients such as hardboiled EGGS (for a variation add a little curry powder), cooked butter BEANS or boiled potatoes.

- Yoghurt sauce can be made by thinning yoghurt with a little single cream or milk, and then flavouring it with a few finely chopped onions or MUSHROOMS which have been gently fried until soft in a little vegetable OIL. To serve all you have to do is reheat the sauce gently (don't let it come to the boil) and pour it over your food. This sauce goes well with most cooked vegetables.

yoghurt

Zest is the strongly flavoured outer part of LIME, LEMON or orange peel. To remove it first scrub the fruit well (to get rid of PESTICIDES) then grate the skin finely.

Zucchini is another name for courgette and courgettes are a variety of small marrow, and a marrow is an edible gourd, which is . . . and so it goes on. Zucchini are used a lot in Mediterranean cooking as they combine well with tomatoes and GARLIC which are popular throughout the area.

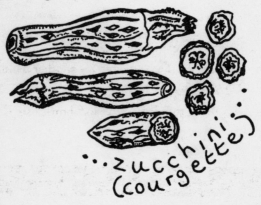

. . . zucchini (courgette)

...recipe...

Zucchini and Zest Spikes (for 4)

2 tablespoons cooking OIL

675 g (1½ lb) zucchini, cut into 'spikes' 5 cm long and ½ cm wide

4 spring onions, washed, dried and chopped

1 red PEPPER, washed, dried and finely chopped

ZEST of 1 LEMON

8 baby SWEETCORN, washed and dried

100 g (4 oz) cashew NUTS

1 tablespoon soy sauce

1) Heat the oil in a large frying pan or wok.

2) Add the zucchini, spring onions, red pepper, lemon zest and sweetcorn. STIR-FRY for 3–4 minutes.

3) Add the nuts and soy sauce, stirring for another minute.

4) Serve on a large plate of noodles.

Get your friends to eat this dish from small bowls using chopsticks.

NOTES